Recreating Yuletides Past

Celebrations of
Yuletide in America before 1860
Recreated at Winterthur

Winterthur Museum and Gardens
Winterthur, Delaware

Harriet Martineau, while in Hingham, Massachusetts, in 1834, wrote, "I was present at the introduction into the new country of the spectacle of the German Christmas-tree. My little friend Charley and three companions had been long preparing for this pretty show. The cook had broken her eggs carefully in the middle for some weeks past, that Charley might have the shells for cups; and these cups were gilded and coloured very prettily.... We were all engaged in sticking on the last of the seven dozen of wax-tapers, and in filling the gilded egg-cups and gay paper cornucopias with comfits, lozenges, and barley-sugar. The tree was the top of a young fir, planted in a tub, which was ornamented with moss. Smart dolls and other whimsies glittered in the evergreen, and there was not a twig which had not something sparkling upon it.... I have little doubt the Christmas-tree will become one of the most flourishing exotics of New-England."—*Retrospect of Western Travel*, 1838.

Introduction

On November 23, 1814, Harriet Manigault of Philadelphia wrote in her journal, "The common question which is now asked in society is 'Do you think we shall have a gay winter... are you not afraid it will be very dull this winter?'" From the early eighteenth century in the southern colonies and, increasingly, throughout all the colonies, the short days of winter became a focal point for social activity. It was true of most affluent Americans who were later joined by a rising middle class. In addition, immigrant groups from central and northern Europe brought traditions that had been long cherished as a means of bringing light and gaiety to the long winter nights. By the nineteenth century many of the social activities melded into one season, from a few days in length to six weeks or so, when Americans of most economic levels and religious persuasions enjoyed the opportunity to share entertainments with their families and neighbors. Harriet Manigault remarked on that November day that she cared not whether the season was full of brilliant parties so long as there were a few that were "very small and consequently more sociable."

In Virginia, by the late eighteenth century, schoolmasters, tutors, and ranking household staff were given one or more bottles of fine brandy as a token of the family's appreciation and respect. And among many slaveholders it was the custom to give farm and household workers new clothes and up to three days off for their own celebrations with music and dance. Many households followed the English custom of "boxing," where each servant, box in hand, would receive an appropriate token in coin from guests and family members.

Some Americans for both religious and economic reasons did not celebrate the holiday season or Christmas Day. Others regarded New Year's Day as the principal occasion for gathering or calling to wish others well. Most activities mixed men and women together, and children were held to limited participation. But there were social times when men and ladies celebrated separately and other occasions when strict rules of behavior governed the social exchange.

Yuletide at Winterthur celebrates the entire social season from early December to the Feast of Epiphany when the great Twelfth Night cake was cut as the highlight to a glittering ball, musicale, or dessert. The Yuletide tour began in 1978 with special evening candlelight tours through twenty period rooms made festive with the addition of greenery and desserts. Since then the tour has become a popular annual event. Guided by the need to understand more fully those early social customs, members of the museum staff searched diaries, journals, personal letters, business accounts, early publications on manners and household management, and contemporary prints, drawings, and paintings to find evidence of both ordinary and special activities of the season. Each year elements are added to the tour as our understanding deepens. Now a tour presentation might include the earliest decorated Christmas tree which can be documented in America; a shooting-in of the New Year; a New Year's calling; a ball with an accompanying late-night dessert; a musicale; a quilting frolic; a gentlemen-only evening of wagers and high spirits; a midday hunters' feast with its preprandial rounds of punch and other spirits; a tutor's schoolroom just before the Christmas recess; or a snowy night in the town square as the last coach arrives.

Recreating Yuletides past is the cumulative work of literally all the members of the Winterthur staff. It is their research, imagination, preparation, and collective efforts that are offered in this booklet. The Yuletide chairmen who have guided this tour to its present state deserve special mention:
Jody Shoemaker, 1978–80;
Susan Burrows Swan, 1980–81;
Phillip Curtis, 1982–84; and
Donald Fennimore, 1987.

E. McSherry Fowble, 1985–86
Peter Hammell, 1978–87

Azalea Woods in winter.

With short and often dark days fading into long evenings, most of the entertainments of the Yuletide season before 1850 were held by candlelight, and numerous candles were required to provide a brilliant effect.

American stage wagon, 1795.—Isaac Weld, *Travels through the States of North America . . . 1795, 1796, 1797.* Eighteenth- and nineteenth-century travelers of some fortune could employ a driver and carriage for themselves or hire one for just the day. Those who traveled on a public conveyance often suffered miserable accommodations. Charging each passenger per mile, usually ten cents, stage drivers, according to John Cogdell in 1808, took "so many as renders it very inconvenient and oppressive to the Ladies & even Gentlemen—they stop also at every tavern on the road—under the pretense of watering their Horses, they go in—& unless some passangers hurry them with a glass of spirits, they hang about and delay you vastly."

"Oysters are eaten raw, broiled on coals, baked with fat and in other ways," reported John David Scherf in 1783 as he traveled through New York and New Jersey. Travelers from Connecticut to Georgia remarked of enjoying this "pleasant" edible and of its abundance in eighteenth-century America.—John David Scherf, *Travels in the Confederation,* 1788.

Blue Staffordshire Room, 1986 Yuletide tour. "I dined at an ordinary, with three or four Connecticut people, on beef, lobster, potatoes, cheese, butter, custards, etc. and as good cider as ever was tasted. The horses and our dinner only cost me five shillings York." So wrote Robert Hunter on October 19, 1785, as he journeyed through New England. Many travelers before 1850 complained of the food and accommodations at American inns, but others found simple, ample fare to satisfy and warm them after the rigors of riding a coach or stage wagon.

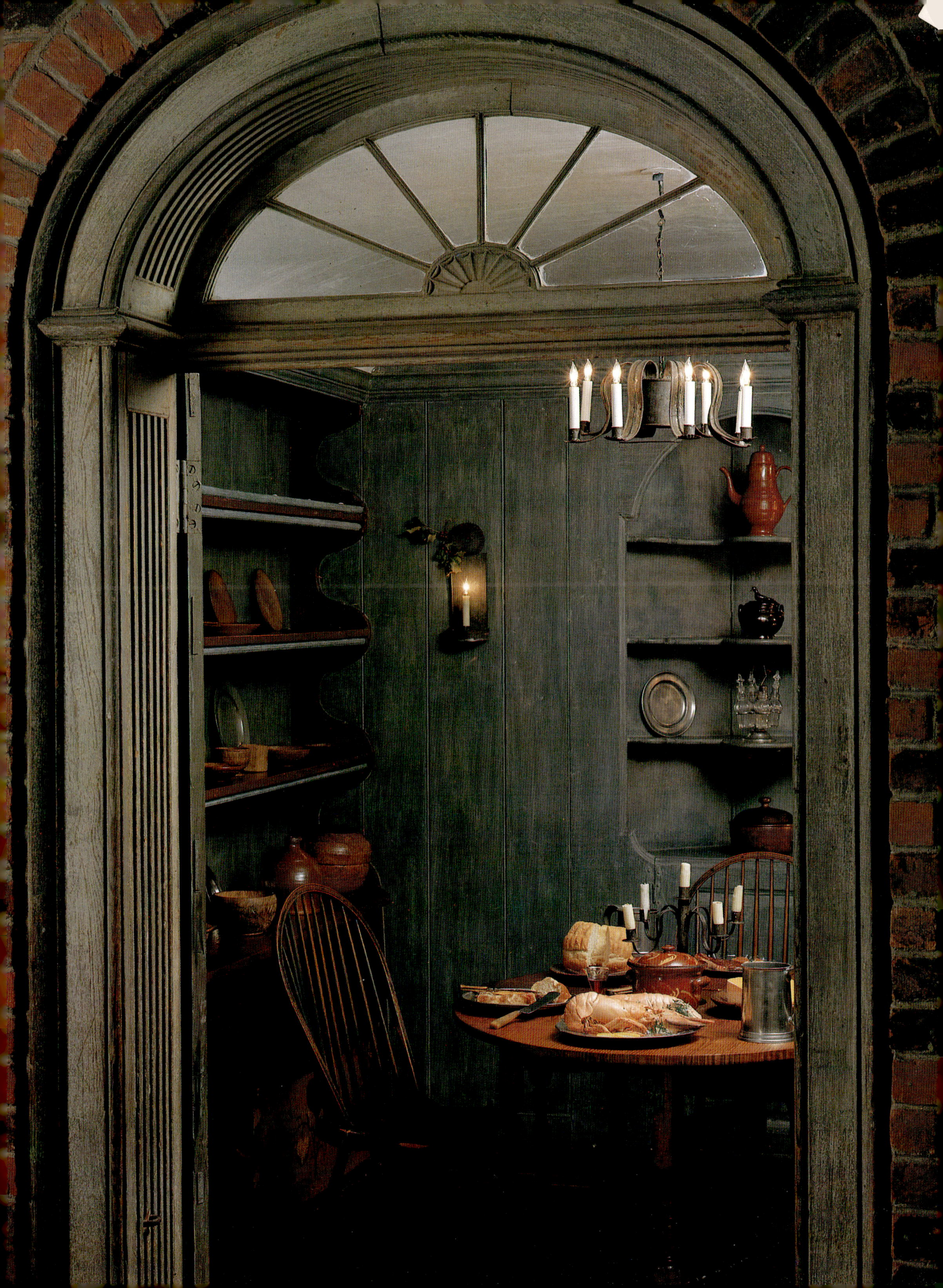

Red Lion Inn, 1986 Yuletide tour. Daily commerce and the demands of those en route to distant family or friends kept wayside inns open on even the darkest nights. Weary travelers found that sleeping arrangements often would huddle the fastidious into the same room, and even the same bed, as the hardworking drivers. Numb from the cold, drivers who had to press on to the next stop could count on temporary relief from a bowl of punch or a pint of ale at each inn.

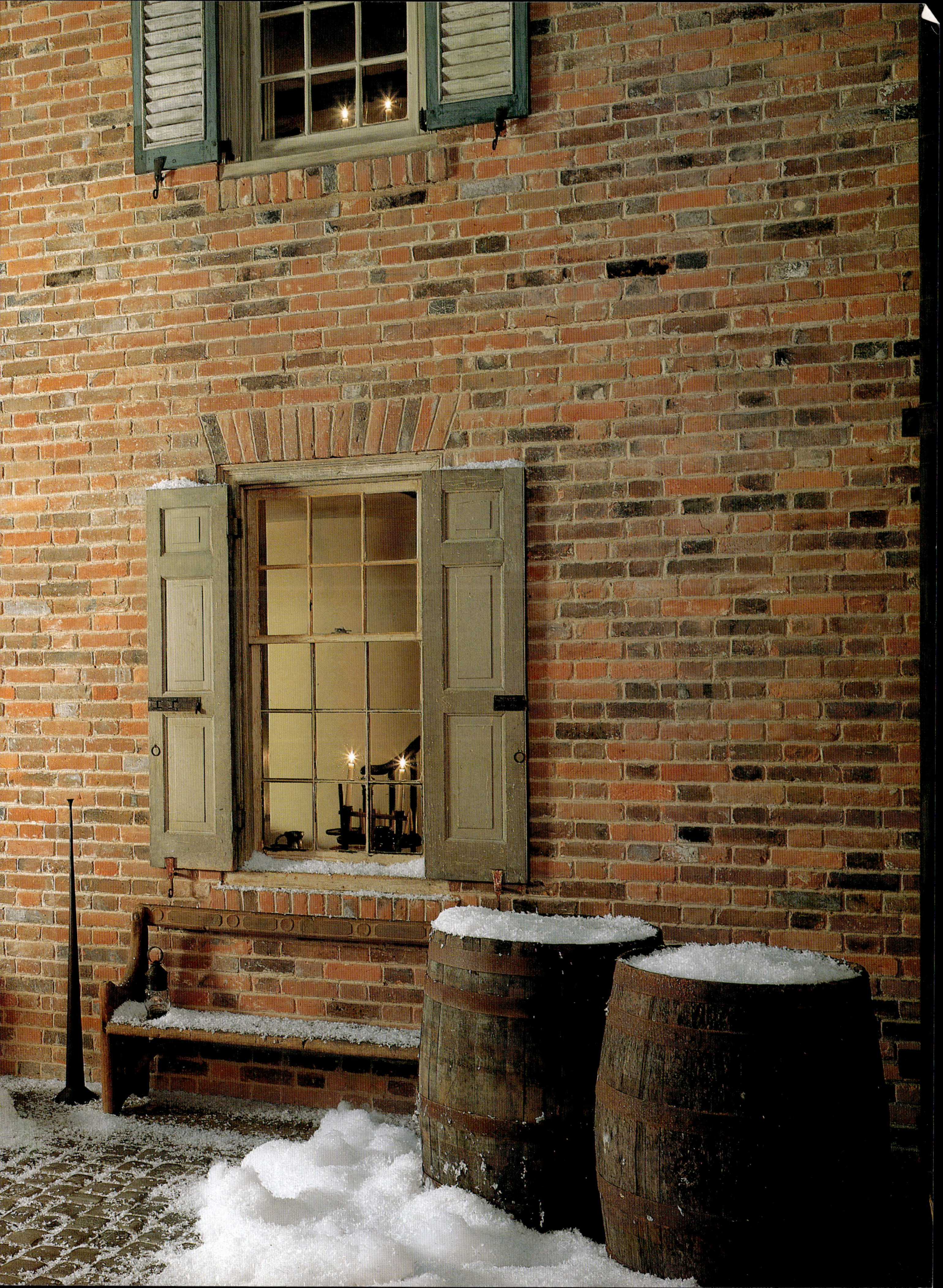

Gate to Pinetum in winter.

Breakfast in the Vauxhall Room, 1986 Yuletide tour. However rigorous the travel, homes of the eighteenth century were frequently filled with family and friends visiting from a distance during the winter. Once settled at their destination, visitors were likely to stay for several days or longer. Early risers often took small breakfasts in their bedchambers. Such meals consisted of cheese, coarse breads, and tea or some other hot beverage. When the numbers were many, guests gathered in an appropriately furnished room. Breakfast fare could include salt fish, eel, tongue, cold ham, cold beef, beefsteaks, eggs, boiled milk, eggnog, wine, ale, and cider.

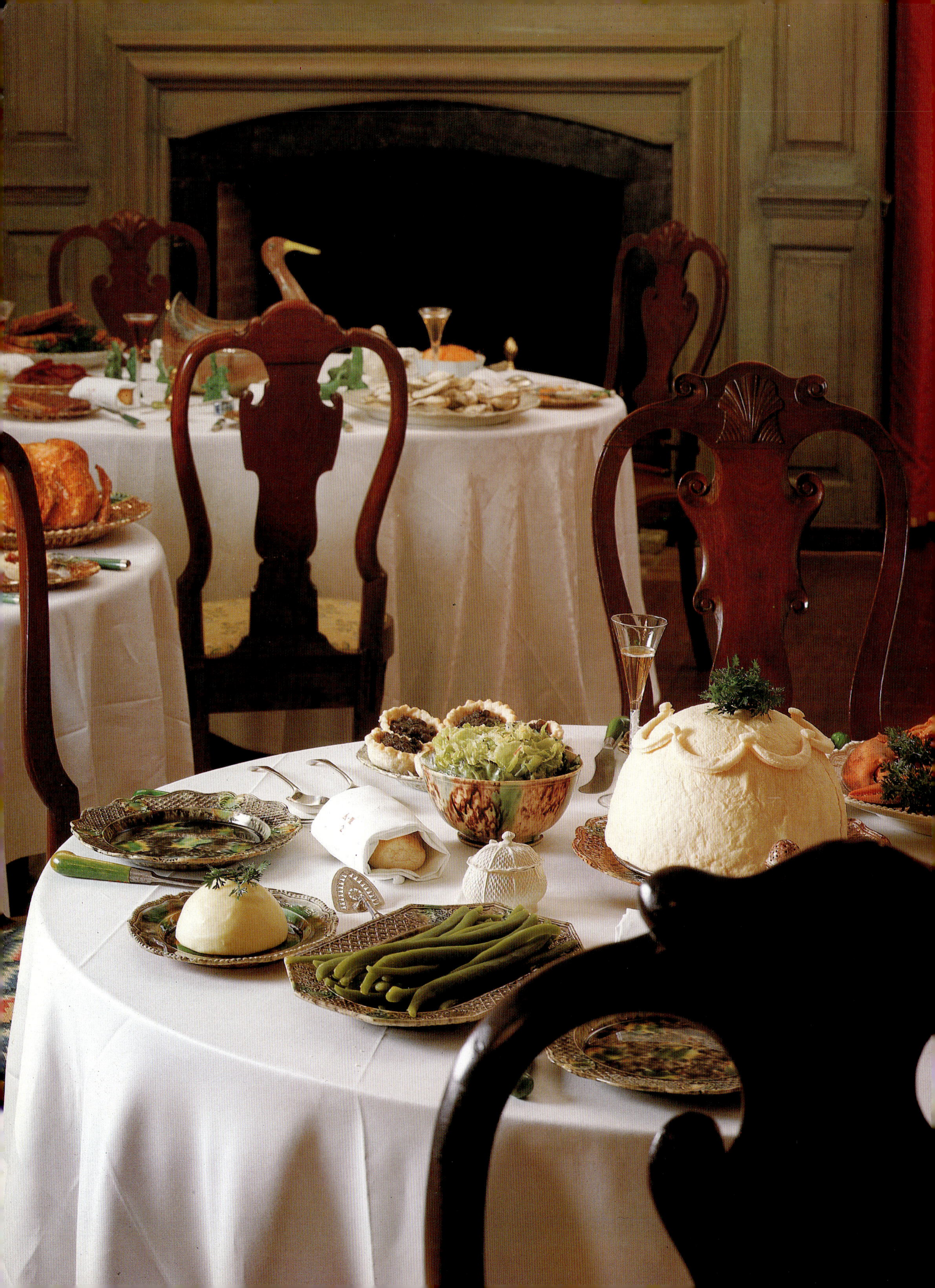

Dinner in the Marlboro Room, 1985 Yuletide tour. The commonest social occasion of the Yuletide season during the eighteenth century was a bounteous dinner for family members, neighbors, and friends. To accommodate large gatherings, the hosts placed several small tables in the largest room. The tables, which seated from four to eight people, were set with linen cloths. A "Great Pie" with an elaborate pastry cover was served during the first course of the meal. Other dishes served with it might include several varieties of fowl, meats, fish, soup, sweets, and vegetables, giving the tabletop a crowded appearance.

Port Royal entrance on the western facade of Winterthur.

Holly leaves and berries on a pie.

Dessert in the Vauxhall Room, 1984 Yuletide tour. Proper eighteenth-century hostesses knew that their dessert table should be centered with a wooden and wicker frame, or dessert board, if they wanted to comply with the instructions offered in a variety of contemporary books. The dessert should be "dressed upon a level" or raised, and the central dish should be higher than the others. Placed on the dessert board and table here are typical early eighteenth-century confects including tarts, preserved fruits, nuts, fresh fruit, and a black-walnut cake. The dessert table also features a tin-glaze earthenware posset pot in the rear right. Curdled possets, an English invention, were made of milk or cream, wine or beer, and spices, sometimes thickened to a custardlike consistency with eggs, bread, barley, or oatmeal. Possets were taken on social occasions or to treat a variety of complaints.

Fruit pies in Pennsylvania German sgraffito plates sit on a table dressed with a handworked tablecloth dated 1824, 1981 Yuletide tour.

Apricot leather in du Pont Dining Room, 1979 Yuletide tour.

15

Drinking, too, had an important place in social interchange, at cards, or after dinner. William Hogarth's print of English gentlemen in the euphoric pursuit of yet another glass of punch was painted in 1732 and issued as an engraving in 1733. From its first issue, *A Midnight Modern Conversation* never failed to amuse and delight Englishmen and Americans alike. Colonial records show this ribald scene to have been the most popular of Hogarth's much applauded works, and both men and women appreciated its wit. Nearly eighty years after the print's first publication, one gentlewoman in Marblehead, Massachusetts, considered a tin-glaze earthenware punchbowl with the *Midnight Modern Conversation* copied thereon to be a family treasure.

"Your Tost [sic] Howarth. Hey to the Midnight—Hark-a-way. Hark-a-way." With such convivial abandon Peter Manigault and his friends, including officers De Mare and Cotymore, Captain Massey, Colonel Robert Howarth, Isaac Codin, and the artist, passed decanters of their favorite libations and prepared to spend a long evening. This ink-and-wash drawing by George Roupill, made about 1760 in South Carolina, suggests a familiarity on the part of the artist with Hogarth's *Midnight Modern Conversation*.

Readbourne Parlor, 1986 Yuletide tour. A frequent accompaniment to simple refreshments or a small meal, the bowl of punch was often centerpiece to an evening's entertainment. Indeed, Americans consumed quantities of alcoholic beverages at breakfast, at dinner, at supper, and in between. Readbourne, the Centreville, Maryland, house of James Holliday, was famous as a site of hospitality from the early 1730s. Set within architecture from the parlor of this house is a recreation of Hogarth's 1733 engraving *Midnight Modern Conversation*.

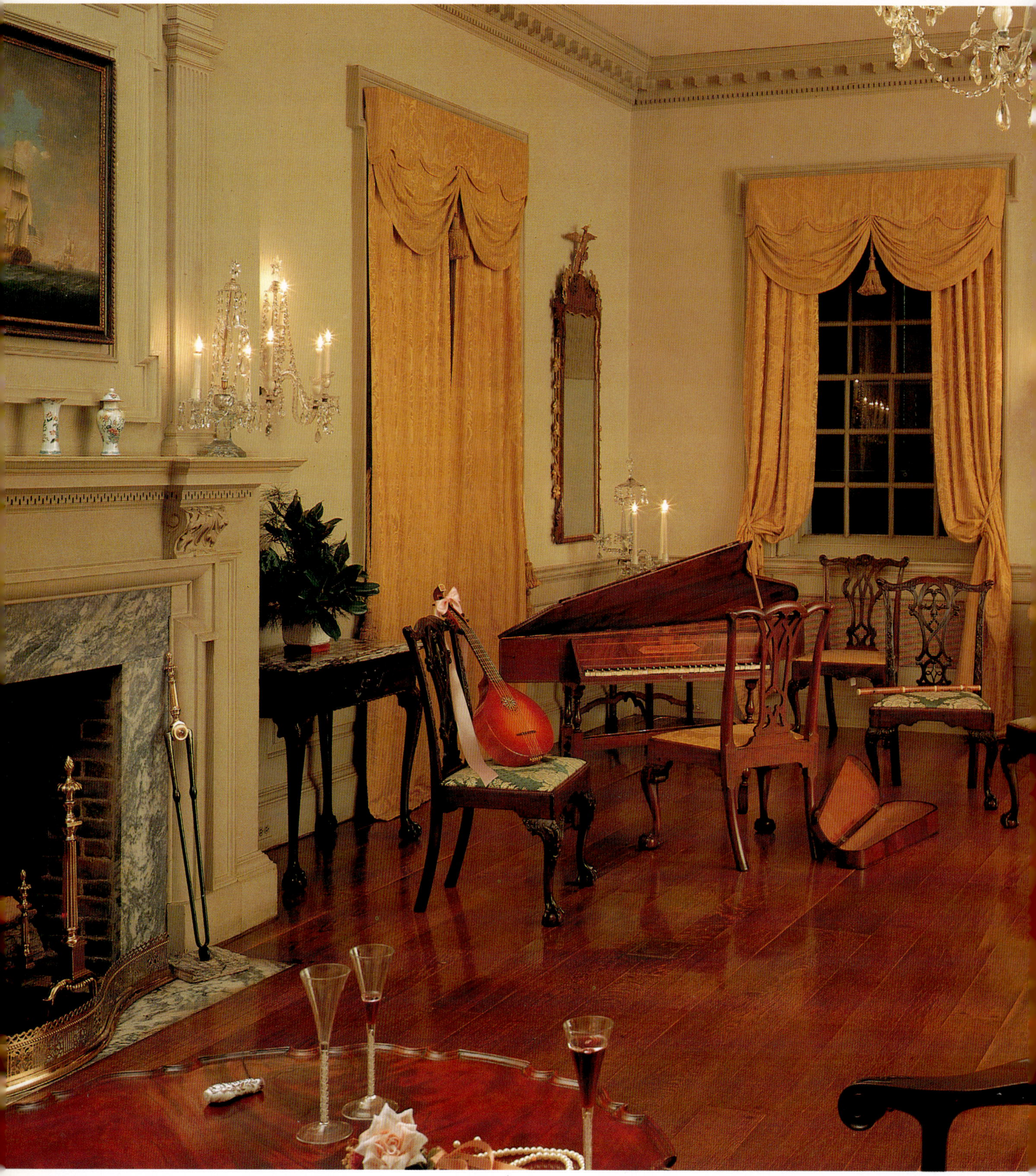

Detail, Port Royal Parlor, 1986 Yuletide tour. Francisco de Miranda wrote in his journal for January 17, 1784, "the dance begins at seven o'clock and lasts until two or three in the morning.... Between eleven and twelve the whole gathering ascends to the hall on the second floor where tea, coffee, and chocolate are served," after which the dancing resumed.

Port Royal Parlor arranged for a ball, 1986 Yuletide tour. A ball was not an impromptu affair. "Preparations begin early in the day when the sofas, chairs and tables should be removed as well as every other piece of furniture which is likely to be in the way or injured.... A ball-room should be brilliantly lighted and this is done in the best style by a chandelier lamp suspended from the center of the ceiling.... Lusters placed on the mantel-piece and branches on tripods in the corner of the room, are also extremely ornamental." Young men and women were taught the more formal figures such as cotillions, minuets, and quadrilles, but they also danced the more exuberant reels and jigs.—William Parks, *Domestic Duties*, 1828.

In 1744 it was observed that those "not Engaged in any Dancing Match might either Employ themselves at Cards, Dice, Back-Gamon, or with a cheerful Glass." Nearly a century later, in 1828, Basil Hall observed, "dancing is the universal amusement, with a couple of wist tables in the Corner for those who are so disposed."

Readbourne Stair Hall set for cards, 1980 Yuletide tour. John Quincy Adams, on December 27, 1786, recorded in his diary, "we convers'd and play'd whist, and sung till 10 o'clock," and a year later remarked of a pleasant evening on December 5 when "Commerce and whist" were played. Commerce is a game characterized by exchanges or bartering. Whist, cribbage, and nearly every table game were subject to the added excitement of wagering.

"Whigs" served on an eighteenth-century English salt-glaze plate.

By the early nineteenth century the pieced quilt was given—and received—as a token of high esteem. Making one required many hours and much skill and was often a group activity. After long hours of cutting, piecing, and sewing, the ladies celebrated with a hearty repast followed by fiddling and dancing. John Lewis Krimmel of Philadelphia illustrated such a scene in his *Quilting Frolic* in 1813.

Mistletoe and evergreen, traditionally associated with the winter-solstice ritual, are shown hanging from the center chandelier and sprigged in individual window lights of an eighteenth-century English tavern. Detail from engraving, *Settling the Affairs of the Nation* (London: Bowles and Carver, 1794–1800).

One Yuletide decoration firmly documented to eighteenth-century English interiors is the bunch of mistletoe suspended overhead. Sprigs of holly, evergreen, and other leafy twigs were also tucked in seemingly unlikely containers such as candlesticks, mortars, and handled pot lids. Engraving, *The Chimney Sweep Giving Betty Her Christmas Box* (London: Bowles and Carver, 1794–1800).

Quilting in the Kershner Parlor, 1986 Yuletide tour. A December quilting party required last-minute efforts of hostess and guests to finish the quilt. Foods, many brought by the quilters to supplement their hostess's board, wait nearby.

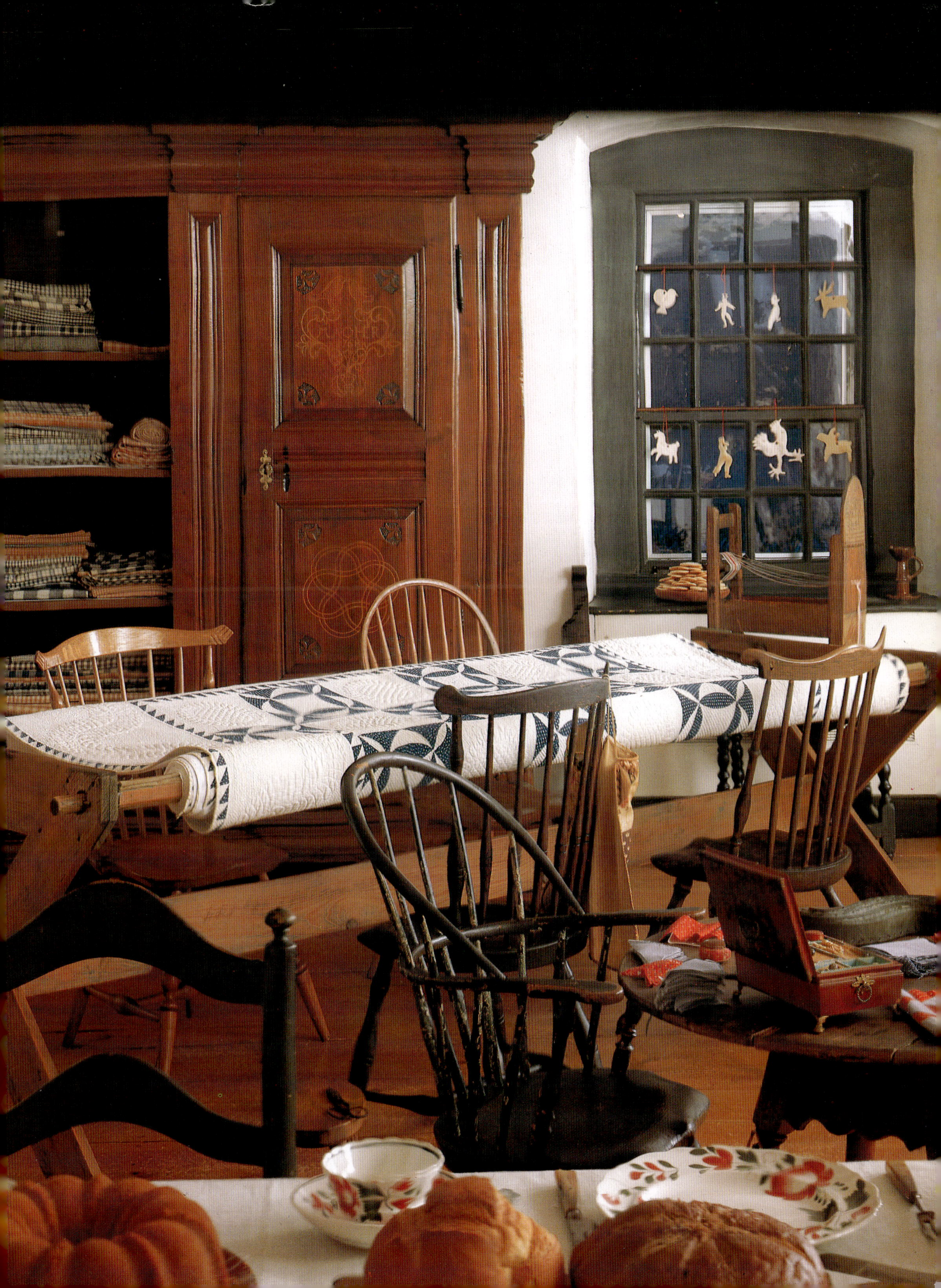

A German Christmas in the Kershner Parlor, 1984 Yuletide tour, is recreated here based on Krimmel's drawing and similar documentation.

By far the most detailed view of an early American Christmas tree is John Lewis Krimmel's wash-and-ink drawing of 1816–20 of a Germantown, Pennsylvania, parlor. A treetop, probably holly or laurel, was festooned with cookies and fruit and placed on a tabletop in front of the fireplace. Beneath the tree is a fenced garden with figures.

German-speaking Protestants who came to America beginning in the late seventeenth century celebrated the Christmas season with candlelight, fellowship, and special sweets to please children and adults alike. Cookies, both delicious and decorative, were cut in traditional shapes of stars, *Belschnickle*, and wreaths and hung as ornaments.

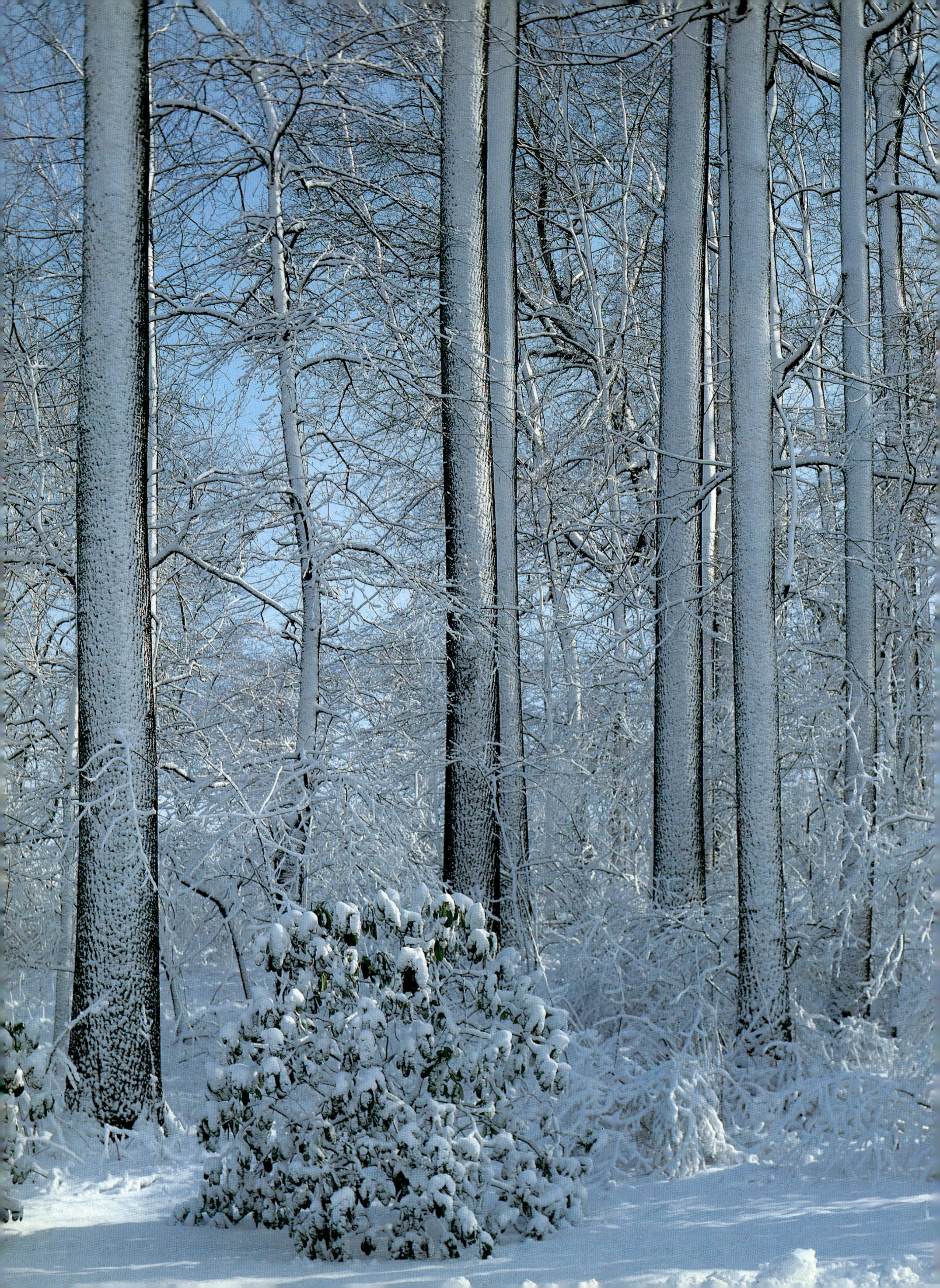

New Year's Day calling, Phyfe Room, 1986 Yuletide tour. "I had an opportunity on New Years' Day of witnessing . . . the Old Dutch custom of running the round of complimentary calls. . . . We must literally run . . . we call on every lady we know, and always find her sitting up . . . with cake and wine on the table."—Adam Hodgson, *Letters from North America*, 1824. "New Year's Day is the most important of the whole year. All of the complimentary visits, fun and merriments of the season seem to be reserved for this day. . . . Having paid our respects . . . wished . . . the compliments of the season, a happy new year, and drunk a glass of excellent punch, we took our leave."—John Lambert, *Travels through Canada and the United States*, 1806.

Azalea Woods after a January storm.

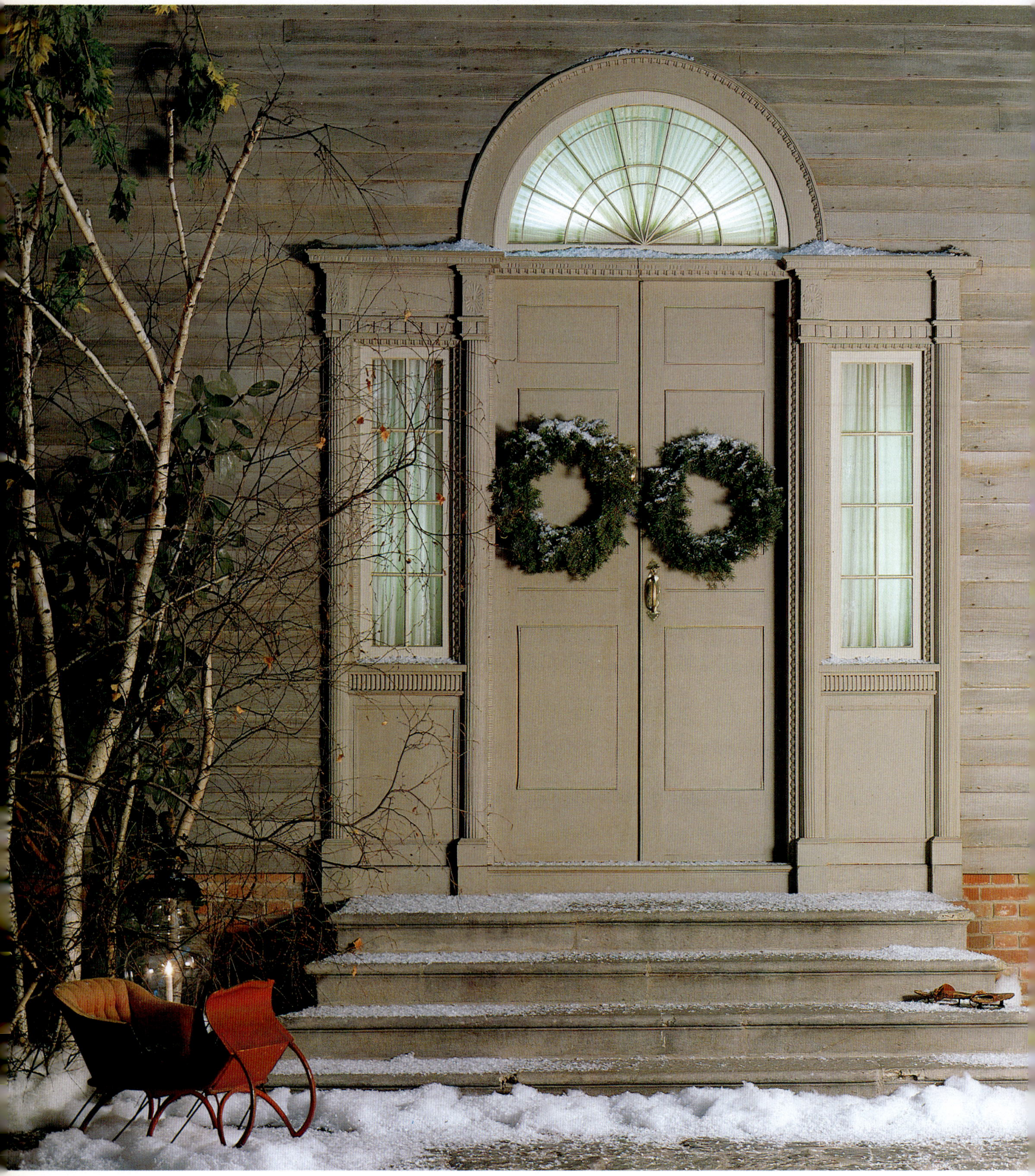

Plants brought indoors to survive the winter gave color and fragrance to some American homes in the eighteenth century. In 1796 Maryland seedsman and florist Peter Billet ordered "60 sorts of double anemonies, 22 sorts carnations, 16 sorts narcissus, all sorts tulip seeds." About the same time Lady Jean Skipwith of Virginia brought inside "Oranges, Lemons and Limes . . . Oleander and Dwarf Myrtle . . . Rose Geranium, and Chrysanthemum Invicum."

The Court: Montmorenci facade, 1986 Yuletide tour.

29

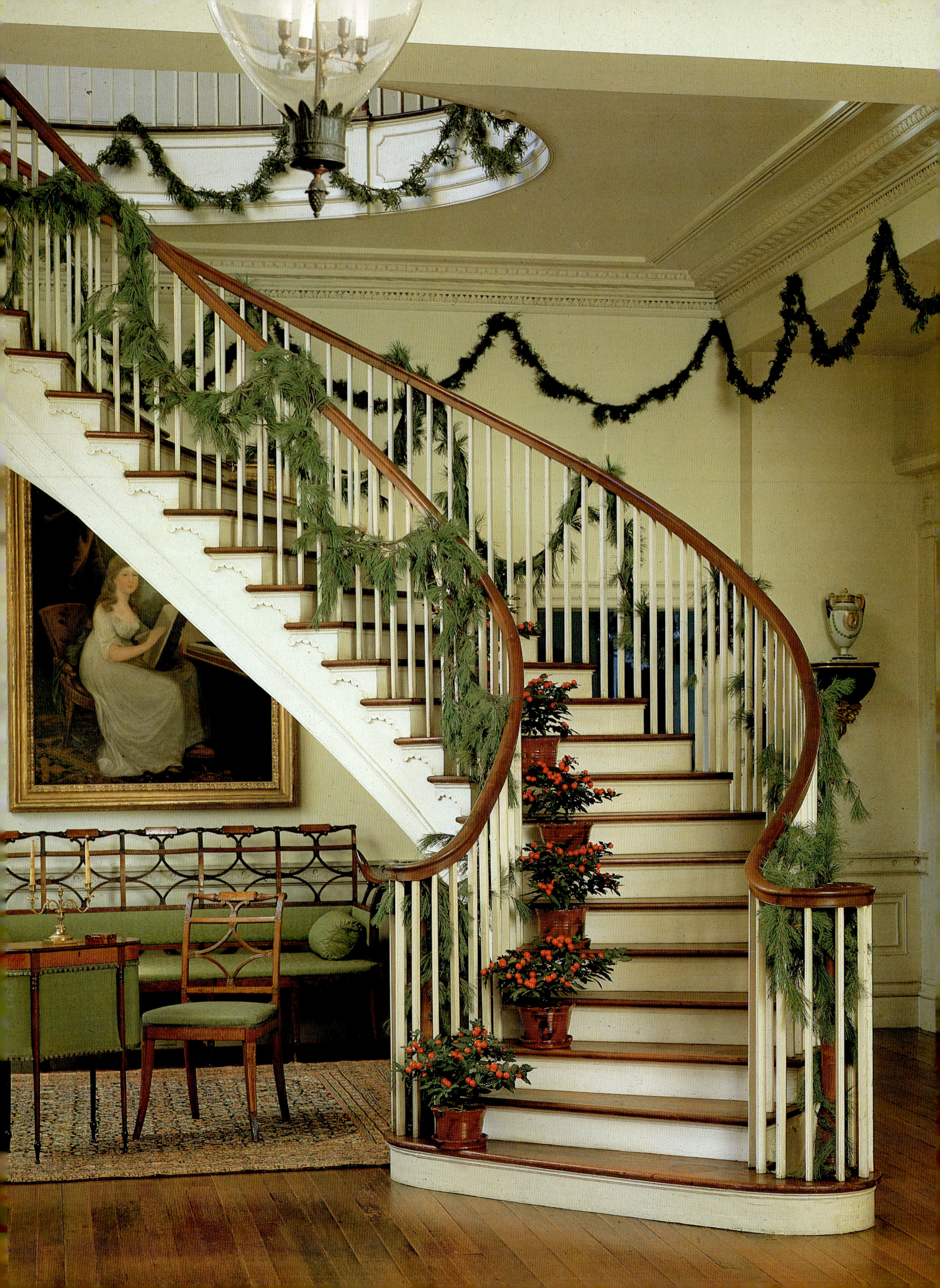

References to December nuptials are found in letters, diaries, and journals, where special fare is very much in evidence. Recipes for bride's and groom's cakes appear in many eighteenth- and nineteenth-century cookbooks. The most spectacular of these had to be the one described by William Wirt, which, reaching nearly four feet in height, is recreated here and reflected in the looking glass in Montmorenci Stair Hall.

Montmorenci Stair Hall decorated with swags of greenery, 1983 Yuletide tour. Eighteenth-century records document the custom of using greens in churches at Christmas, particularly in Anglican churches. In 1834 Harriet Martineau wrote that the church in Hingham, Massachusetts, was "dressed up with evergreens in great variety, and arranged with much taste." She also observed in the same year, "at home the rooms were prettily dressed with greens and an ample supply of lights provided against the evening."

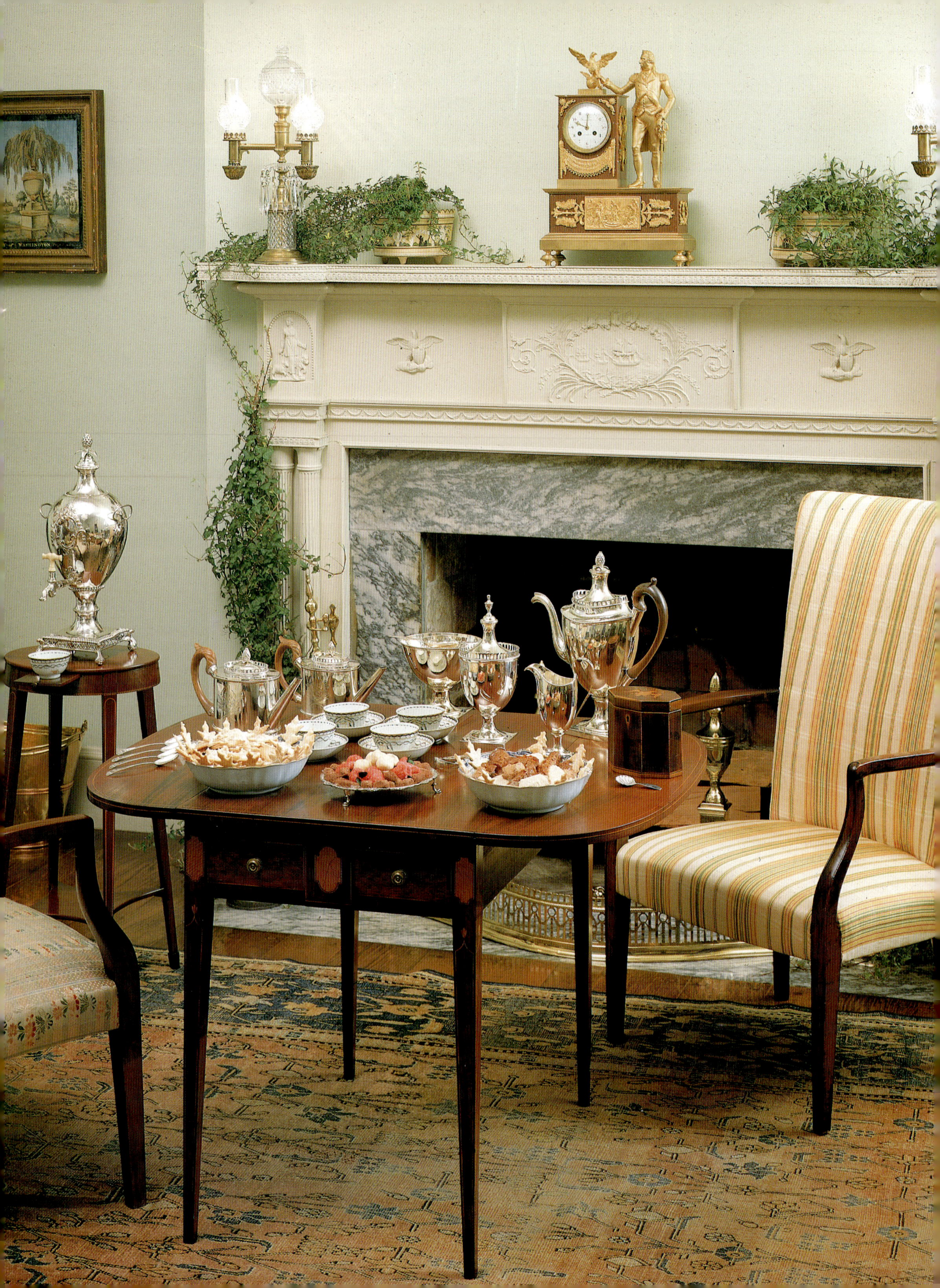

Silk flowers in Montmorenci Stair Hall, 1986 Yuletide tour. By the second half of the eighteenth century silk flowers were the point of fashion in Europe. Ladies used them to adorn their gowns and hair and particularly to decorate dessert displays. Silk-flower arrangements also gained support in both Europe and America. The arrangement here, based on flower paintings of the early nineteenth century, is set in a *famille verte* vase made in China, 1770–1800.

Baltimore Drawing Room set for tea, 1986 Yuletide tour. Tea parties, in the afternoon or early evening, were fashionable during the Yuletide season in the eighteenth and early nineteenth centuries. As the hostess presided over her tea table, she mixed strong tea, water, sugar, and cream to suit the taste of each guest.

Gifts were given and received through New Year's Day. Gentlemen who rushed from house to house, hostess to hostess, to extend greetings received in turn small tokens, among them paste baskets filled with sweetmeats. Twenty-one-year-old Harriet Manigault remarked of the gifts exchanged in her family and with friends between Christmas and New Year's Day 1814: "We must now get something ready for new years day. We have already begun to distribute Xmas boxes & I am very much pleased with what I received." On the twelfth day, Friday, January 6, she added, "friends sent us some little notes in answer to ours. Christmas was this."

Guest Sitting Room, 1985 Yuletide tour. "The stockings were hung by the chimney with care, in hopes that St. Nicholas soon would be there." Clement Moore's verse of 1823 still gives hope to children that by some stroke of good fortune their stockings will be stuffed full of delectables. The stocking crammed to its limits with small gifts clearly was not the sole province of the young. In 1810 a broadside commissioned by John Pintard served as an invitation to the first annual dinner of the St. Nicholas festival in New York City. It featured a large, filled stocking as a principal motif.

A German Christmas in the Fraktur Room, 1980 Yuletide tour. John Lewis Krimmel's sketch of a Pennsylvania German family's Christmas celebration is the basis for this recreation. A child's long list of wants is in a prominent place next to a fruit- and confection-laden tree and a boot stuffed with good things to eat. Nearby, a bundle of switches gives an all-too-clear warning to naughty children.

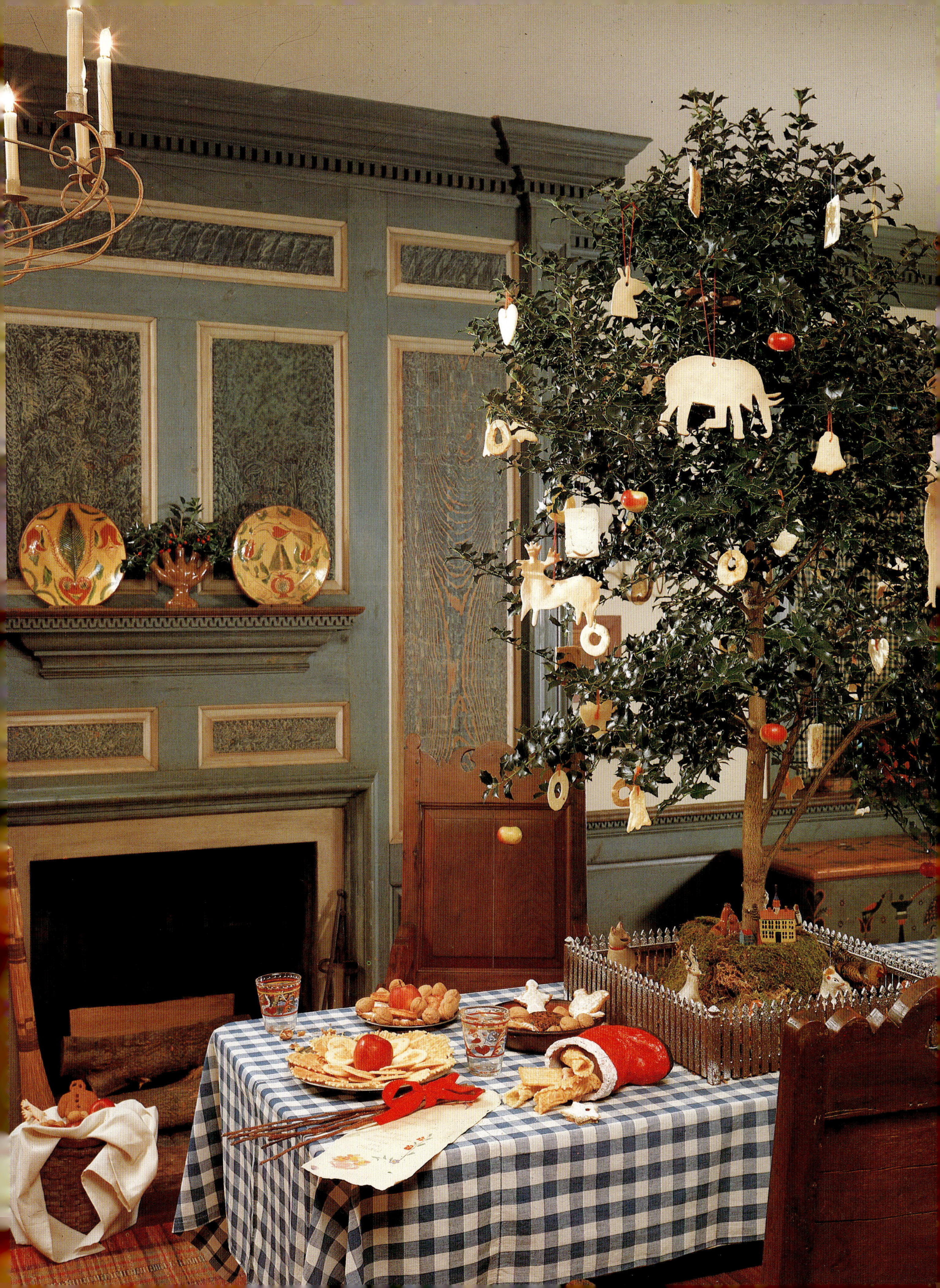

View from Pinetum in winter.

Twelfth Night cake, Port Royal Entrance Hall, 1985 Yuletide tour. "Last night I went to the Ball. It seems this is one of their annual Balls supported in the following manner: A large rich cake is provided and cut into small pieces and handed around to the company, who at the same time draws a ticket out of a Hat with something merry wrote on it. He that draws King has the Honor of treating the company with a Ball the next year, which generally costs him Six or Seven Pounds. The Lady that draws the Queen has the trouble of making the Cake."—*Journal of Nicholas Cresswell*, entry for January 7, 1775, Alexandria, Virginia.

Empire Parlor set for a musicale, 1986 Yuletide tour. On December 20, 1843, Henry Whipple went to a "candy party" at the home of a friend. During the evening the party was entertained by some "sweet music" on the piano. Most educated young people played one or more instruments and, judging from the remarks of diarists and journalists, were quite eager to perform, whether for an evening of dancing or for an elaborate dessert.

Holiday preparations in the Kershner Bakehouse and the Kershner Kitchen, 1979 Yuletide tour.

Twentieth-century Americans are usually surprised to learn that the celebration of New Year's was far more commonly observed in the eighteenth century than was the celebration of Christmas. One popular manner of marking the passage of the old year into the new was by "shooting in the New Year." The young men of a community would go from farm to farm to welcome the new year. At each house one of the company would chant a special poem called the "New Year's Speech." Members of the party would fire their guns in succession in a salute to the family and then be invited inside for food and drink.

Conservatory, 1986 Yuletide tour. Traditionally an eighteen-foot Christmas tree decorated in the "old-fashioned" manner with multicolored lights, tin reflectors, glass ornaments, and tinsel filled the center of the Winterthur Conservatory during the family's residence. In recent years the Conservatory tree has been decorated with flowers collected from the fields and cutting gardens at Winterthur, dried, and tied in colorful bunches.

Cover inset and title page:
The poinsettia is associated with the Yuletide season, both at Winterthur and in homes throughout America, but by historical standards this tradition is fairly recent. The familiar red-and-green plant was first introduced into the United States only a few years after German families in Pennsylvania decorated the earliest Christmas trees recorded in America. Other customs that we regularly associate with this winter season began much earlier and, like the poinsettia and the decorated evergreen tree, have grown in importance and elegance.

Published 1987 by
The Henry Francis du Pont
Winterthur Museum, Inc.
Winterthur, Delaware 19735
All rights reserved.
No part of the contents of this book may be reproduced without written permission.
Designed by Paulhus Associates
Printed in Japan
ISBN 0-912724-18-8
Photo credits
Philip G. Correll, p. 4
Gottlieb Hampfler, p. 26
Ian M. G. Quimby, p. 13 top